Towards a Conservative Sociology

CHARIT GUPTA

TABLE OF CONTENTS

ABOUT THE AUTHOR

Charit Gupta is a passionate scholar and emerging expert in the field of Conservative Sociology. Currently pursuing his academic journey at Jawaharlal Nehru University, Gupta has dedicated his studies to exploring the intricate dynamics of tradition, values, and societal norms in contemporary contexts.

With a profound curiosity for understanding how conservatism shapes our societies, Gupta's research has brought new perspectives to the forefront of social science. His work delves deep into the often-neglected aspects of conservatism, shedding light on its profound influence on modern life.

In this compelling collection of essays, Gupta invites readers to embark on a journey through the intricate tapestry of *Conservative Sociology*. His thought-provoking insights challenge conventional wisdom and spark conversations about the enduring relevance of tradition in today's rapidly changing world.

1

Introduction: The Significance of a Conservative Sociology

Conservative sociology is an academic field that focuses on understanding society through the lens of traditional values and principles. It seeks to analyze social structures, institutions, and behaviors from a conservative perspective, emphasizing the importance of continuity, stability, and order. This essay aims to explore the key principles and concepts of conservative sociology and its contribution to our understanding of society.

Sociology, as a discipline, has long been devoted to unraveling the intricate fabric of society, seeking to decipher its inner workings and dynamics. Within this vast field of study, there exists a niche, a perspective that champions the enduring values and principles that have molded our societies across generations. This perspective is known as *Conservative Sociology*, and its significance lies in its unique approach to comprehending the complex tapestry of human existence.

Conservative sociology, as an academic discipline, offers us a distinct lens through which to examine society. It is an intellectual vantage point that places traditional values, principles, and norms at its core. In doing so, it delves deep into the essence of continuity, stability, and order—qualities that have been fundamental to the human experience for centuries.

At its heart, *Conservative Sociology* seeks to preserve and celebrate the legacies of the past, acknowledging that the lessons of history provide valuable insights for navigating the present and shaping the future. It is a discipline that asks us to pause and reflect on the enduring wisdom of our forebears, recognizing that, amidst the rapid changes of our world, there is enduring value in the traditions that have withstood the test of time.

This essay endeavors to shed light on the key principles and concepts that underpin *Conservative Sociology* and elucidate its profound contribution to our understanding of society. Through a thoughtful exploration of its tenets, we hope to unveil the intricate connections between tradition and societal structures, institutions, and behaviors. By the essay's conclusion, we aim to have not only grasped the significance of this unique perspective but also to appreciate its role in shaping our perception of the world we inhabit. In doing so, we embark on a journey of intellectual discovery, guided by the principles of continuity, stability, and order.

To understand the significance of our discipline, it's necessary to delve into its core principles:

Preservation of Tradition: *Conservative Sociology* places a premium on preserving and upholding the traditions, customs, and values that have been passed down through generations. It asserts that these traditions hold inherent wisdom and are essential for maintaining social stability.

Social Continuity: This perspective emphasizes the importance of continuity in social structures and institutions. It contends that abrupt and radical changes can disrupt the fabric of society, leading to instability and disorder. *Conservative Sociology* seeks to analyze how these continuities shape our lives.

Stability and Order: The pursuit of stability and order is central to *Conservative Sociology*. It posits that societies thrive when there is a degree of predictability and orderliness in the social, political, and economic realms.

Community and Solidarity: *Conservative Sociology* places a strong emphasis on community and social cohesion. It argues that a sense of belonging and shared values fosters cooperation and harmony within society.

Resistance to Rapid Change: This perspective tends to be cautious about rapid societal change. It believes that sudden shifts in values and institutions can have unintended consequences, and therefore, it advocates for a measured and reflective approach to change.

Balanced Perspective: By focusing on tradition and stability, *Conservative Sociology* provides a counterbalance to more progressive or radical viewpoints. It encourages a nuanced understanding of society that recognizes the merits of continuity alongside the need for evolution.

Cultural Preservation: This perspective champions the preservation of cultural heritage and indigenous knowledge, helping safeguard the diverse traditions that enrich our global tapestry.

Social Critique: *Conservative Sociology* doesn't shy away from critiquing aspects of society that may undermine stability or erode traditional values. It offers a critical lens to evaluate the consequences of rapid change.

Policy Implications: Understanding the principles of *Conservative Sociology* can inform policy decisions. Policymakers may consider the potential impact on tradition and stability when implementing reforms or introducing new policies.

Historical Context: This perspective reminds us of the historical context in which societies have evolved. It encourages us to appreciate the significance of historical continuity in shaping the present.

In short, *Conservative Sociology* significance resides in its commitment to understanding society through the lens of tradition and stability. By exploring its principles and concepts, we gain valuable insights into the delicate balance between preserving the past and adapting to the future, ultimately contributing to a more comprehensive understanding of the complex societies in which we live.

2

THE IMPORTANCE OF TRADITION IN SOCIETY

a) Tradition: The Pillar of Stability; b) Traditional Values and Their Role in Social Cohesion; c) Examining the Evolution of Tradition

a) Tradition: The Pillar of Stability

Tradition plays a crucial role in society, serving as a guiding force that provides continuity, stability, and a sense of identity. It encompasses a range of cultural, social, and religious practices that are passed down from generation to generation. Conservative sociology recognizes the significance of tradition in shaping social structures and behaviors, and emphasizes its value in maintaining social cohesion and stability.

Tradition offers a shared framework of values, beliefs, and customs that bind individuals together. It provides a sense of belonging and identity, helping individuals situate themselves within a larger social context. Traditional practices, rituals, and celebrations strengthen social bonds, fostering a sense of unity and solidarity among community members. By adhering to established traditions, individuals find stability, predictability, and a sense of purpose in their lives.

Furthermore, tradition serves as a repository of accumulated wisdom. It represents the collective knowledge, experiences, and insights of previous generations. Traditional practices often embody practical solutions and time-tested approaches to social, cultural, and moral challenges. By drawing upon the lessons of the past, societies can avoid repeating past mistakes and find guidance in navigating contemporary issues.

b) Traditional Values and Their Role in Social Cohesion

Traditional values are the bedrock of social cohesion, serving as the cultural glue that binds communities and societies together. These values encompass a range of principles, such as respect for authority, honor, loyalty, and a strong sense of duty towards one's family and community.

At their core, traditional values provide a shared ethical framework that guides individual behavior and interactions. They offer a collective moral compass, helping individuals navigate complex social situations while maintaining a sense of cultural identity and belonging.

One of their fundamental roles is to establish social norms and expectations. These norms define what is considered acceptable behavior within a given society, promoting consistency and predictability in human interactions. This predictability reduces the potential for conflict and fosters a sense of security.

Traditional values also emphasize the importance of collective responsibility. Individuals are encouraged to fulfill their roles and duties within the family and community, contributing to the common good. This collective responsibility nurtures cooperation, mutual support, and a strong sense of solidarity among community members.

Furthermore, traditional values often prioritize long-term stability and harmony over short-term individual desires. They encourage individuals to consider the impact of their actions on the broader community, reinforcing the idea that social bonds and interdependence are essential for the well-being of everyone.

Moreover, traditional values often prioritize the welfare of the group over individual desires. This emphasis on communal well-being promotes cooperation, mutual support, and solidarity within communities. It encourages individuals to contribute to the common good and helps establish a sense of interdependence among community members.

In summary, traditional values serve as a moral and ethical foundation that underpins social cohesion. They provide a sense of identity, establish norms, encourage collective responsibility, and promote cooperation, all of which are essential elements in fostering strong, stable communities and societies.

c) Examining the Evolution of Tradition

Tradition, as a concept, is often associated with stability, continuity, and the preservation of values and practices passed down through generations. However, it is crucial to recognize that tradition is not a static entity but a dynamic force that evolves over time in response to changing circumstances, values, and social dynamics. In this chapter, we will delve into the intricate process of how tradition evolves, adapts, and continues to shape societies.

While tradition provides stability and continuity, it is not static. It reflects the collective experiences and values of a particular community or culture. As societies evolve and encounter new challenges, traditions undergo transformations to remain relevant. These adaptations can be subtle or profound, but they are essential for tradition's continued existence.

Cultural shifts play a pivotal role in the evolution of tradition. When societies experience changes in demographics, technology, or global influences, traditional practices may be reinterpreted or modified to accommodate these shifts. For example, traditional family structures may evolve to encompass diverse family forms as societal norms change.

Tradition and modernity are not necessarily in opposition but often coexist in complex ways.

Modernity brings new ideas, technologies, and global perspectives, which can both challenge and enrich tradition. In some cases, traditions adapt to modernity, incorporating new elements while retaining their core values. This interplay creates a dynamic tension that shapes cultural landscapes.

Generational shifts influence how tradition evolves. Younger generations may reinterpret traditional practices in light of their own experiences and values. This process can lead to innovations within tradition while preserving its essence.

Globalization has accelerated the exchange of ideas and cultures, impacting traditional practices. While globalization can lead to the erosion of certain traditions, it can also facilitate the sharing and preservation of traditions on a global scale. Many traditional practices find new audiences and appreciation through international exposure.

Tradition's ability to evolve and adapt is a source of strength for societies. It allows communities to draw upon their cultural heritage when facing challenges, providing a sense of continuity and stability in uncertain times. This adaptability is exemplified by how traditional healing practices have been integrated into modern healthcare systems.

The evolution of tradition is not without its challenges and controversies. Striking a balance between preserving cultural heritage and accommodating change can be complex. Some argue that rapid modernization threatens the integrity of tradition, while others believe that adaptation is essential for tradition's survival.

Tradition is a living and evolving entity that reflects the ongoing story of human societies. Its fluidity and adaptability ensure its relevance and resilience in an ever-changing world. Embracing the evolution of tradition allows us to appreciate the dynamic nature of culture and the rich tapestry of human heritage. As we move forward, we must continue to study and cherish tradition's capacity to provide stability, continuity, and a sense of identity while embracing the innovations and adaptations that shape our shared global culture.

Conservative sociology recognizes the importance of tradition in shaping social structures, values, and behaviors. Traditional values play a crucial role in maintaining social order, promoting social cohesion, and fostering a sense of collective responsibility. By examining the evolution of tradition, conservative sociologists gain insights into how societies adapt while preserving core values.

3

ORGANIC SOCIETY: THE INTERCONNECTED WEB OF RELATIONSHIPS

a) Society as an Organic Entity; b) The Concept of Social Cohesion; c) Exploring the Bonds That Hold Communities Together

a) Society as an Organic Entity

Analogous to a living organism, society operates as an organic entity. Just as a body is composed of various interconnected parts working together for the overall health and well-being, society is composed of diverse individuals, communities, and institutions that are interdependent and contribute to the functioning of the whole.

This perspective highlights that society is more than a mere collection of isolated individuals pursuing their self-interests. Rather, it emphasizes the intricate network of relationships and the collective actions that shape social order. Understanding society as an organic entity allows sociologists to analyze the reciprocal influences between individuals and their social environment.

Much like a living organism, society is seen as a complex and interconnected system with various components that work together to maintain stability and order. In this view, different social institutions, such as family, religion, government, and the economy, are akin to organs within the societal body, each serving a distinct yet interdependent function.

One of the key principles derived from this analogy is the importance of maintaining equilibrium and homeostasis within society. Just as a living organism strives to keep its internal environment stable, society seeks to achieve and preserve a state of balance. Any disruption or change within one part of society can have far-reaching consequences, much like an imbalance in an organism's systems can lead to illness or dysfunction.

Conservative sociology places a strong emphasis on stability, continuity, and the preservation of traditional values and institutions. It contends that these elements are vital for the well-being of society, akin to the preservation of essential organs and functions in a living organism.

Furthermore, this perspective tends to resist rapid or radical change, as such changes are viewed as potentially disruptive to the overall health and stability of society. Instead, it advocates for a measured and gradual approach to societal changes, emphasizing the importance of preserving established norms and traditions.

The organic analogy also underscores the notion of collective identity and solidarity. It highlights the interconnectedness of individuals within a society and their shared sense of belonging. Similar to how cells in an organism work together for the organism's survival, individuals in society are encouraged to cooperate and maintain a sense of unity for the greater good.

A conservative sociology must critique what it

perceives as social pathologies or disruptions to the social organism. These pathologies can include rapid social change, breakdowns in traditional institutions, or moral decay, which are seen as harmful to the overall health of society.

The concept of society as an organic entity provides a theoretical framework for understanding how conservative thinkers view the interconnectedness, stability, and continuity of society.

b) The Concept of Social Cohesion

Social cohesion is a central concept within the framework of an organic society in conservative sociology because it serves as the vital glue that holds the social organism together. In this perspective, social cohesion represents the harmonious functioning of different societal parts, akin to the synchronized operation of various organs in a living organism.

Within an organic society, social cohesion is seen as essential for maintaining stability and order. Just as the proper functioning of organs and systems in a living organism ensures its overall health, social cohesion ensures the health of the societal body. When individuals and groups within society cooperate and adhere to shared norms and values, it contributes to a sense of unity and collective identity.

Social cohesion reinforces the idea that individuals are interconnected and interdependent. When individuals feel a strong sense of belonging and shared purpose, they are more likely to work together for the common good, just as different parts of an organism collaborate for its survival.

Moreover, social cohesion contributes to the preservation of tradition and the continuity of societal norms and values. It ensures that the transmission of cultural heritage and traditional practices remains intact, as individuals are more likely to uphold and pass down these elements when they feel a sense of cohesion and belonging to their cultural or social group.

In the context of an organic society, social cohesion acts as a stabilizing force. It helps mitigate conflicts and tensions, reducing the potential for societal disruptions. When individuals are bound together by a shared sense of identity and responsibility, they are more likely to resolve disputes amicably and maintain social order.

Overall, within the framework of an organic society in conservative sociology, social cohesion is a central concept because it represents the cohesive and harmonious functioning of societal components, mirroring the coordinated operation of organs in a living organism. It underscores the importance of unity, cooperation, and shared values in maintaining societal stability and continuity.

c) Exploring the Bonds That Hold Communities Together

Conservative sociology explores the various bonds that contribute to social cohesion and hold communities together. These bonds can be categorized into multiple dimensions:

Cultural Bonds: Shared language, customs, traditions, and shared history contribute to a collective cultural identity that binds individuals within a community. Cultural bonds foster a sense of belonging and provide a foundation for social solidarity.

Relational Bonds: Relationships within families, friendships, and community networks play a crucial role in maintaining social cohesion. Strong interpersonal connections create a support system, encourage cooperation, and contribute to a sense of trust and belonging.

Institutional Bonds: Institutions, such as religious groups, schools, and local community organizations, provide a sense of structure and collective purpose. They promote social integration, facilitate the transmission of values and knowledge, and create spaces for shared experiences and collective action.

Economic Bonds: Economic relationships and interdependencies, including labor markets, trade networks, and communal economic endeavors, contribute to social cohesion by fostering cooperation, interconnectivity, and shared prosperity.

Conservative sociology analyzes the interplay between these different dimensions of bonds within communities, in order to understand how they contribute to stability.

Exploring the various bonds that hold communities together provides insights into the dynamics of social order and the factors that contribute to a cohesive and thriving society. Through a comprehensive analysis of an organic society, conservative sociologists gain a deeper understanding of the interdependence among individuals, communities, and institutions, leading to a more nuanced understanding of social dynamics.

4

THE FAMILY: CORNERSTONE OF SOCIETY

a) Understanding the Traditional Family Structure; b) Gender Roles and Family Dynamics; c) The Impact of Family on Individual Development

a) Understanding the Traditional Family Structure

Towards a conservative sociology, traditional family structure holds a pivotal role, regarded as a foundational unit of society. This conventional family arrangement typically features a married heterosexual couple and their children, each member fulfilling well-defined roles and responsibilities. Within this framework, the family plays a multifaceted role in fostering social continuity.

One of the primary aspects that must be underscored is the family's function as a source of stability. It provides a secure and nurturing environment for the upbringing of children. The presence of a committed marital relationship within this structure is believed to offer a sturdy foundation for the emotional and psychological development of the young ones. This stable family environment is considered indispensable for the well-being and growth of children.

Furthermore, the family serves as a crucial agent for the transmission of cultural values. It acts as the initial conduit through which individuals are introduced to their cultural heritage, language, customs, and belief systems. This early exposure to cultural values helps shape an individual's sense of identity and belonging, reinforcing the perpetuation of cultural traditions across generations.

Within the traditional family, conservative sociology often advocates for clearly defined roles and responsibilities for family members. This may include a division of labor, where the husband and wife have distinct roles and duties. Such divisions can reflect traditional gender roles, with the husband typically seen as the primary breadwinner and the wife as the primary caregiver and homemaker. This division is considered conducive to family stability and efficiency.

Within the framework of conservative sociology, the traditional family structure is highly regarded as a foundational unit of society. It is seen as providing not only a stable and nurturing environment for child-rearing but also as a key vehicle for the transmission of cultural values and the perpetuation of social traditions. The adherence to clearly defined roles and responsibilities within this family structure is seen as a means of maintaining order and stability within society.

b) Gender Roles and Family Dynamics

Gender roles play a significant role within the family, shaping the dynamics of relationships and responsibilities. Conservative sociology acknowledges the complementary nature of gender roles, arguing that they contribute to the overall well-being and functioning of the family unit.

The division of labor based on gender roles allows for specialization and cooperation within the family. It recognizes and values the unique contributions that each gender brings to the family unit. Gender roles provide a framework for successful family functioning, as they reflect natural and inherent differences between men and women.

A conservative sociology, while emphasizing the significance of the traditional family structure, also recognizes the importance of flexibility and adaptation within this framework to accommodate evolving societal norms and individual preferences. It acknowledges that the traditional family can and should adjust to changing circumstances while preserving its core principles as a foundational unit of society.

Within this perspective, the recognition of flexibility means that the traditional family structure can adapt to modern realities. It acknowledges that societal norms are not static and that family arrangements can evolve over time. For example, it acknowledges the changing roles of men and women in the workforce and the need for flexibility in how family responsibilities are shared.

Additionally, conservative sociology respects the autonomy and individual preferences of family members. It acknowledges that not all families will adhere rigidly to traditional gender roles or family structures. Instead, it allows for variations that reflect the unique needs and choices of the individuals within the family.

At the same time, conservative sociology emphasizes the importance of maintaining the core principles of the family unit. These principles often include values such as commitment, stability, and the nurturing of children. While the structure of the family may adapt to changing circumstances, these principles remain fundamental to the family's role in society.

It's important to recognize that the traditional family structure can evolve and adapt to contemporary realities while still upholding its essential role in providing stability, nurturing, and cultural transmission within society. It balances the need for flexibility with the preservation of core family values and principles.

A conservative sociologist must be critical of what

he perceives as the modern destructuration of the family. This perspective argues that the traditional family structure, characterized by a married heterosexual couple with well-defined roles, is a cornerstone of societal stability and continuity. From this perspective, the modern shift away from traditional models can be problematic for several reasons.

First and foremost, the traditional family structure is viewed as a stable and nurturing environment for raising children. It provides a framework in which children can develop emotionally, socially, and psychologically. Deviations from this structure may lead to disruptions in the well-being of children, as they may not benefit from the stability and support that the traditional family offers.

Moreover, the traditional family has historically been considered the primary vehicle for transmitting cultural values and traditions. It serves as the initial context in which individuals are introduced to their cultural heritage, language, and customs. Departing from this structure may raise concerns about the potential loss of cultural continuity and identity.

Conservative sociology also argues that the destructuration of the family can contribute to social instability. They contend that when traditional family values erode, it can lead to a breakdown in social cohesion and a sense of shared responsibility. This, in turn, may result in an increase in social issues such as delinquency, substance abuse, and family instability.

The modern destructuration of the family must be rejected, because the traditional family structure ais a bedrock of stability, cultural continuity, and social order. While acknowledging the importance of adaptability to changing societal norms, this perspective maintains that the traditional family structure should be preserved to ensure the well-being of individuals and the cohesion of society.

c) The Impact of Family on Individual Development

The family is undeniably a potent force in shaping the development of individuals. It serves as the primary socializing agent, molding the values, attitudes, and behaviors of its members. Conservative sociologists place great emphasis on the family's role in this process, arguing that a stable and nurturing family environment is paramount for the overall well-being and socialization of individuals.

Within the family, individuals are first introduced to the fundamental values and beliefs that will guide their lives. These values often reflect the cultural, religious, and moral principles of the family and community. Conservative sociologists assert that a stable family provides a structured and consistent environment for the transmission of these values, allowing individuals to develop a strong ethical foundation.

Moreover, the family is where individuals learn the dynamics of interpersonal relationships. It is within the family that people acquire essential social skills, such as communication, empathy, and cooperation. The quality of these early social interactions significantly influences how individuals navigate relationships in other spheres of life. A stable and nurturing family environment is seen as crucial in fostering healthy interpersonal skills.

The family also plays a pivotal role in imparting a sense of identity and belonging. It provides individuals with a cultural and familial context, helping them understand their place in the world. Conservative sociologists argue that the family's stability and continuity contribute to a strong sense of identity and connectedness, reinforcing an individual's sense of purpose and community.

Furthermore, the family can be a source of emotional support and security. It serves as a sanctuary where individuals can seek solace, share their joys and sorrows, and receive unconditional love and care. A stable family environment is believed to offer, indeed, emotional stability, contributing to an individual's mental and emotional comfort.

When the family structure becomes destabilized or undergoes significant change, it can have adverse effects on individual development. Disruptions within the family, such as divorce or shifting gender roles, can lead to uncertainty, stress, and a diminished sense of security for family members, particularly children.

The family's profound influence on individual development highlights its role as a primary socializing agent. The preservation of a stable and nurturing family environment contributes significantly to the overall well-being, values, and socialization of individuals within society.

5

COMMUNITY: THE POWER OF LOCAL CONNECTIONS

a) Importance of Local Communities; b) Social Support and Collective Action; c) Preserving Community Identity and Values

a) Importance of Local Communities

Local communities hold a profound significance within the realm of social organization, serving as fundamental units that shape the lives of individuals. These communities are not merely geographical entities but rather intricate networks of relationships, shared experiences, and common interests. Conservative sociologists and others emphasize the pivotal role of local communities in society, as they provide a range of benefits that extend far beyond their physical boundaries.

At their core, local communities offer individuals a sense of place, belonging, and identity. They provide a geographic and cultural anchor in an increasingly globalized world. Within these communities, individuals find a physical space they can call home, surrounded by people who share similar experiences, values, and traditions. This sense of place and belonging fosters a deep connection to one's surroundings, instilling a feeling of rootedness that is vital for personal well-being and identity formation.

Local communities are not just geographical entities but also social ones. They function as sources of support and mutual assistance, forming tight-knit social networks that extend beyond immediate family ties. In times of need, whether due to personal crises or broader societal challenges, these communities often come together to provide help, comfort, and solidarity. This support system bolsters individuals and families, creating a safety net that contributes to social stability and resilience.

Moreover, local communities facilitate social integration. They offer spaces for interaction, collaboration, and shared activities, cultivating a sense of interconnectedness among their members. Whether through local schools, religious institutions, or community events, individuals within these communities have opportunities to engage with others, form friendships, and build a sense of common purpose. This social integration contributes to a stronger sense of community identity and shared values.

In an era marked by increased mobility and digital connectivity, local communities play a crucial role in counterbalancing the potential disconnection from one's immediate surroundings. As people navigate global networks and digital spaces, local communities provide a tangible and intimate sense of connection to the physical world. They offer a respite from the fast-paced, often impersonal nature of modern life, allowing individuals to engage in face-to-face interactions, strengthen community bonds, and celebrate shared traditions and customs.

Local communities serve as foundational units of social organization, offering individuals a sense of place, belonging, and identity. They provide a support system that extends beyond family, promote social integration, and maintain a sense of rootedness in an increasingly interconnected world. As vital sources of connection, local communities contribute significantly to the well-being and social fabric of society, highlighting their enduring importance in the human experience.

b) Social Support and Collective Action

In human existence, local communities weave together the lives of individuals through shared experiences, mutual assistance, and enduring connections. These communities, often defined by geographical proximity, offer far more than mere geographical boundaries; they are the lifeblood of social support systems. Within their confines, individuals find a network of relationships that can offer not only emotional solace but also practical and material assistance during times of need.

At the heart of local communities lies the strength of social bonds. These bonds transcend mere acquaintance, evolving into profound relationships that often resemble familial ties. In these circles, individuals find friends who become like family, confidants who offer a listening ear, and allies who stand by their side through life's ups and downs. It is within these relationships that the foundations of social support are laid.

Perhaps one of the most defining characteristics of social support within local communities is the provision of emotional sustenance. When individuals face the dark clouds of personal crises—be it the loss of a loved one, the weight of a health issue, or the turmoil of emotional distress—the community becomes a sanctuary of empathy and understanding. Neighbors, friends, and fellow community members offer not just comforting words but also a profound sense of shared experience. This emotional support serves as a crucial lifeline, helping individuals navigate life's tumultuous waters while safeguarding their mental and emotional well-being.

Yet, social support within local communities extends beyond emotional sustenance; it encompasses practical assistance as well. When life presents its inevitable challenges, whether in the form of unforeseen emergencies, financial hardships, or the daily grind of existence, the community emerges as a wellspring of practical help. A neighbor may step in to babysit for a family in crisis, a friend might offer a ride to medical appointments, or a group of community members might organize meal deliveries during a challenging period. These acts of kindness and assistance lighten the burdens that individuals and families bear, reinforcing the bonds of solidarity and reciprocity within the community.

In times of crisis, material resources often make a significant difference in the lives of those facing adversity. Local communities frequently unite to pool resources, whether through charitable donations, volunteer efforts, or the establishment of community organizations. These resources can take the form of food banks, clothing drives, or financial assistance programs that provide tangible support to those in need. The availability of such resources underscores the value of local networks as a safety net for vulnerable individuals and families, ensuring that they do not bear their burdens alone.

The social support networks within local communities go beyond crisis intervention; they contribute to a broader sense of belonging and identity. Community members do not merely receive support; they actively engage in giving back to the community. This reciprocity strengthens the sense of community identity and shared values, fostering a spirit of cooperation and mutual assistance that benefits everyone. It is within these communities that individuals find not just a place to reside but a place to truly belong.

The resilience of local communities becomes especially apparent when facing adversity. Whether in the form of natural disasters, economic downturns, or public health crises, the bonds forged within these communities are put to the test. However, it is often within the local community that individuals discover the resources and collective determination required to weather these challenges and emerge stronger on the other side. The sense of unity and mutual support that characterizes these communities contributes to their resilience in the face of adversity.

Local communities offer to individuals a lifeline of emotional solace, practical assistance, and material resources during times of need. The bonds formed within these communities reflect the strength of human connections and the enduring importance of community in the intricate tapestry of human existence. As pillars of social support, local communities not only provide assistance but also nurture a profound sense of belonging, identity, and resilience that enriches the lives of all who are part of them.

c) Preserving Community Identity and Values

Local communities stand as guardians of community identity and values, cradling collective memories, shared traditions, and ethical compass that guide their members. This duty places local communities at the heart of preserving the cultural and moral foundation of society.

Cultural preservation takes center stage within these communities. They are not passive observers of history, but living custodians of heritage. It is here that time-honored customs, rituals, and folklore find not only safekeeping but vibrant continuation. From celebrating ancient festivals with fervor to nurturing linguistic traditions and preserving culinary customs, local communities ensure that their cultural identity remains not as a relic, but as a living, breathing force in the lives of their members.

Embedded within this cultural preservation is a commitment to transmitting knowledge from one generation to the next. Elders become revered sources of wisdom, passing down stories, values, and traditional skills to the young. The oral traditions that thrive within local communities are the threads that connect the past to the present.

Values, too, find their sanctuary within these circles. Local communities are bastions of moral principles and ethical codes, encouraging the virtues that bind their members together. They instill a sense of responsibility, accountability, and respect for others, shaping not only individual characters but also the collective conscience of the community.

In times of rapid change and uncertainty, local communities offer a steady anchor. They remind individuals of who they are, where they come from, and the values that anchor their lives. This sense of continuity provides a source of comfort and stability in an ever-evolving world.

As custodians of community identity, local communities are entrusted with a profound responsibility. They are the keepers of the flame, ensuring that the cultural heritage and moral foundations of society remain relevant. In doing so, they not only honor the past but also provide a compass for the future, guiding their members on a path of shared identity and enduring values.

6

ORDER AND AUTHORITY: THE FOUNDATION OF STABILITY

a) The Role of Hierarchy in Society; b) Maintaining Social Order; c) The Rule of Law and Its Significance

a) The Role of Hierarchy in Society

Sociology must cast a discerning eye on the concept of hierarchy within the social organization. Hierarchy, in this context, embodies the presence of diverse strata of authority, power, and responsibility that exist within a society. It is not merely an arbitrary arrangement but rather a fundamental component essential for the harmonious functioning and coordination of social systems.

At its core, hierarchies carve out well-defined channels of authority, creating a structured framework within which society operates. These structured tiers of authority do more than merely delegate power; they furnish a scaffold for decision-making processes and the execution of collective objectives. By doing so, hierarchies instill a sense of order, which is crucial in preventing the cacophony of chaos that might otherwise ensue in a society without structure.

Hierarchies serve as the architecture of accountability. Each rung of authority comes with its corresponding set of responsibilities, ensuring that individuals are answerable for their actions and decisions. This not only fosters transparency but also cultivates a culture of responsibility, where individuals understand the consequences of their choices within the broader societal context.

Specialization, a hallmark of hierarchical systems, allows individuals to concentrate on their areas of expertise. In this division of labor, the intricate interplay of skills and knowledge becomes apparent. Specialization is vital for optimizing efficiency: when individuals can focus on tasks where they excel, the overall productivity of society is enhanced.

Moreover, hierarchies facilitate coordination on a grand scale. Think of it as a symphony where each instrument plays a distinct part, yet together they create a harmonious composition. In a similar vein, hierarchies ensure that different components of society work in concert, synchronizing their efforts toward common goals. This orchestration is particularly vital in complex societies where numerous individuals, organizations, and institutions must cooperate to achieve collective objectives.

In the eyes of conservative sociologists, hierarchies are not inherently oppressive or unfair. Rather, they are the organizational scaffolding upon which society's aspirations are built. They view hierarchies as tools that, when designed and managed wisely, can promote cooperation, efficiency, and collective welfare. In this sense, hierarchy is not a mere feature of society but a foundational element that contributes to its stability and functionality.

b) Maintaining Social Order

Maintaining social order is a foundation of any stable and functioning society, and hierarchies, order, and authority are the linchpins that uphold this essential foundation. Within this framework, maintaining social order is not merely a desirable outcome but an absolute necessity for the well-being and continuity of a community.

Hierarchies establish a clear and structured system of authority, providing society with the organizational framework needed to prevent chaos and disorder. At the heart of these hierarchies are well-defined lines of authority, which enable decision-making processes, allocation of responsibilities, and implementation of collective goals.

The structure that hierarchies bring to society is instrumental in upholding social order. It delineates roles and responsibilities, creating a sense of accountability among individuals and institutions. This accountability ensures that actions have consequences, which, in turn, discourages behavior that could disrupt the established order. Within this context, hierarchies become a means of maintaining not only order but also justice and fairness.

Furthermore, the division of labor and specialization, inherent within hierarchical systems, contributes to social order by optimizing efficiency.

When individuals are allowed to focus on tasks aligned with their expertise, productivity increases, and the likelihood of errors or inefficiencies decreases. This efficiency enhances the overall functioning of society, reducing the potential for disruptions that can arise from disorganization or inefficiency.

Order and authority, in the eyes of conservative sociologists, create a stable environment where individuals can pursue their objectives, knowing that societal rules and norms are in place to maintain balance and protect their interests. Social order fosters a sense of security and predictability, enabling individuals to plan for the future.

It's important to stop thinking of hierarchies as oppressive mechanisms, but rather as tools for cooperation and coordination. They are designed to ensure that authority is exercised responsibly and fairly, with the ultimate aim of promoting the common good.

In conclusion, maintaining social order relies heavily on the presence of hierarchies, which provide structure, accountability, and efficiency needed to uphold stability within society. From this perspective, social order is not an abstract concept but a tangible outcome of a well-organized and hierarchically structured community, where individuals can live, work, and thrive in a secure and predictable environment.

c) The Rule of Law and Its Significance

The Rule of Law, from a conservative sociological perspective, embodies a profound commitment to upholding time-tested traditions and values. It serves as a shield against capricious actions by those in authority, ensuring that established customs and norms are preserved. This commitment to continuity and preservation is at the heart of conservative thought, as it guards against the rapid erosion of cultural identity and social stability.

One of the central roles of the Rule of Law, within this perspective, is to protect the sacred rights and liberties of individuals within the framework of tradition. It acts as a bulwark against government overreach and excessive intervention into the lives of citizens, preserving the sanctity of personal freedoms while respecting the boundaries set by societal customs.

The Rule of Law, through its commitment to established norms and practices, contributes to the maintenance of societal order and the preservation of traditional hierarchies. It ensures that authority is exercised in accordance with long-standing values and principles, which in turn reinforces the social fabric and prevents upheaval.

This conservative interpretation of the Rule of Law underscores the importance of the family as a foundational unit of society. The Rule of Law seeks to protect and nurture the traditional family structure, recognizing it as the bedrock of social stability and continuity.

In this perspective, the Rule of Law is a guardian of the past, a steward of the present, and a protector of the future. It reflects a commitment to upholding the principles of tradition, authority, and individual liberties, ensuring that these values remain intact for future generations.

7

SOCIAL CHANGE: BALANCING PROGRESS AND TRADITION

a) Evaluating the Need for Social Change; b) The Dangers of Rapid Transformations; c)Navigating Change while Preserving Stability

a) Evaluating the Need for Social Change

The concept of social change is an ever-present force in the dynamics of human societies. As the world evolves, so too do the values, norms, and structures that underpin our collective existence. However, in the midst of this relentless march forward, it is prudent to advocate for a cautious and thoughtful approach when assessing the need for social change. In our pursuit of progress, we must carefully balance the preservation of tradition, community cohesion, and the potential unintended consequences that may accompany rapid change.

Social change, undoubtedly, has been a force for good throughout history. It has been the catalyst for societal advancements in many areas, and a testament to human ability to learn from the past while shaping a brighter future. However, it is this very potential for profound transformation that necessitates a cautious approach.

First and foremost, tradition is a repository of wisdom, a distilled essence of collective experiences passed down through generations. It encompasses cultural values, customs, and practices that have withstood the test of time. While not immune to evolution, traditions provide a sense of continuity and identity within societies. When advocating for social change, it is paramount to recognize and respect these traditions, understanding that they have often evolved over centuries in response to societal needs and conditions.

Additionally, rapid and abrupt social change can lead to fragmentation and division within communities. Societies are, at their core, networks of relationships, and when change occurs too swiftly or disruptively, it can fracture these bonds. A thoughtful approach to social change recognizes the importance of maintaining social cohesion, understanding that abrupt shifts can leave individuals feeling disoriented and disconnected from their communities.

Unintended consequences are another consideration when contemplating social change. Well-intentioned efforts to address one issue may inadvertently create new challenges or exacerbate existing ones. A cautious approach involves careful examination and evaluation of potential consequences, allowing for adjustments and mitigations to be put in place.

Furthermore, it is essential to involve all segments of society in discussions about social change. A thoughtful approach embraces inclusivity, seeking input from diverse perspectives and engaging in open dialogue. This inclusivity ensures that the voices of all community members are heard, and that the impacts of change are considered from multiple angles.

By striking a balance between progress and tradition, we can navigate the complexities of social change with a measured and conscientious approach, ensuring that the fabric of society remains strong even as it evolves. But it's crucial to exercise caution and thoughtfulness in this pursuit: tradition, community cohesion, and the potential for unintended consequences must all be carefully weighed and considered.

b) The Dangers of Rapid Transformations

The dynamics of social change are intrinsic to the evolution of societies throughout history. As communities progress and adapt to shifting circumstances, they inherently grapple with the intricate balance between embracing new ideas and preserving longstanding traditions. It's within this complex interplay that the dangers of rapid transformations become evident.

Social change, undoubtedly, has the potential to bring about significant advancements and improvements in various facets of society. However, in the zeal to propel change forward, there is a need for mindfulness, for the path of rapid transformation carries its own set of perils.

One of the foremost dangers of rapid social change is the potential erosion of tradition and the wisdom embedded within it. Tradition represents the cumulative wisdom of generations, encapsulating cultural values, customs, and practices that have endured through time. While not impervious to adaptation, traditions offer a sense of continuity and identity within societies. Swift and unconsidered change can lead to the loss of these valuable traditions, disconnecting individuals from their cultural roots and heritage.

Moreover, the fracture of social cohesion is

another peril that accompanies rapid transformations. Societies are fundamentally networks of relationships, interwoven through shared values and experiences. When change is implemented abruptly or disruptively, it can sever these bonds, leaving individuals feeling isolated and adrift. The resulting disorientation can have profound social consequences, including heightened levels of stress, anxiety, and alienation.

Unintended consequences also loom large in the shadow of rapid social change. Well-intentioned efforts to address one issue may inadvertently create new challenges or exacerbate existing ones. It's essential to recognize that change rarely occurs in isolation, and the repercussions can ripple through multiple facets of society. A thoughtful approach to social change involves a comprehensive examination of potential consequences, allowing for adjustments and mitigations to be put in place.

The dangers of rapid social transformation are not to be underestimated. Preservation of tradition, maintenance of social cohesion, and consideration of unintended consequences should all be integral to the process of change. By navigating the complexities of social transformation with care and thoughtfulness, societies can strive for progress while safeguarding the foundational values that define them.

c) Navigating Change while Preserving Stability

Defending tradition while navigating change and preserving stability is akin to walking a tightrope between the past and the future. It's a delicate dance that societies engage in when they seek to honor their cultural heritage while also adapting to evolving circumstances. This approach reflects an understanding that tradition is not static, but a living force that can coexist with progress and change.

Tradition, in its essence, embodies the collective wisdom and shared experiences of generations. It represents the values, customs, and practices that have been passed down over time. These traditions are often deeply intertwined with a society's identity and serve as a source of continuity, anchoring individuals to their cultural roots.

However, the world is in a constant state of flux. Technological advancements, shifting demographics, and changing global dynamics continuously reshape the social landscape. In the face of these changes, societies must decide how to uphold their traditions while adapting to new realities.

Defending tradition in this context does not necessarily mean resisting change at all costs. Rather, it involves a thoughtful and measured approach that allows for the preservation of core values and customs while recognizing that some adjustments may be necessary for a society to thrive in the modern world.

Preserving stability is a fundamental concern when considering the coexistence of tradition and change. Rapid and chaotic transformations can destabilize societies, leading to confusion, conflict, and the erosion of social bonds. The careful navigation of change involves ensuring that the foundations of stability remain intact even as adaptations are made.

One way to achieve this delicate balance is through the process of informed and inclusive decision-making. When societies engage in open dialogues that involve all segments of the population, they can better understand the potential implications of change and work together to find solutions that align with their core values.

Furthermore, it's essential to recognize that tradition itself can evolve. Just as societies adapt to new circumstances, so too can traditions be reinterpreted and reinvigorated to remain relevant. Tradition need not be static; it can be a dynamic force that continues to guide and inspire while embracing the opportunities that change brings.

In conclusion, defending tradition while navigating change is a complex endeavor that requires careful consideration and inclusivity. Tradition is a valuable asset that can provide a sense of identity and continuity, but it should not be an impediment to progress. By striking a balance between honoring tradition and embracing change, societies can evolve while safeguarding the values that define them. It is through this delicate dance that they can forge a path toward a more stable and harmonious future.

8
INSTITUTIONS: GUARDIANS OF TRADITION

a) Government and Its Role in Upholding Tradition; b) Education: Transmitting Cultural Values; c) Religion: The Moral Compass of Society

a) Government and Its Role in Upholding Tradition

In the intricate web of societal structures, institutions preserve and perpetuate values, norms, and customs that define a culture. Among these institutions, government plays a pivotal role in upholding tradition, as it wields the power to shape and reinforce the foundational principles that bind a society together.

Tradition, in its essence, is the accumulated wisdom of a society, encapsulating its historical experiences, cultural heritage, and shared values. Government, as the central institution of authority within a nation, plays a crucial part in safeguarding and nurturing these traditions.

One of the fundamental roles of government in upholding tradition is the preservation of cultural heritage. This involves not only the protection of historical landmarks, artifacts, and cultural practices but also the promotion of cultural education and appreciation through initiatives such as museums, cultural festivals, and educational programs.

Furthermore, government plays a vital role in maintaining and enforcing legal frameworks that protect and promote tradition. This includes legislation that safeguards cultural practices, languages, and historical sites. Additionally, it may involve measures to combat cultural appropriation or disrespect, ensuring that traditions are treated with the reverence they deserve.

Government also serves as a unifying force within society, fostering a sense of national identity rooted in tradition. Through symbols, anthems, and national celebrations, governments can help cultivate a shared identity that is deeply connected to the traditions and values of a nation. This sense of identity can serve as a powerful bond that unites citizens across diverse backgrounds.

Moreover, government has a responsibility to ensure that tradition is not stifling or exclusionary. It must strike a delicate balance between preserving tradition and respecting the rights and values of individuals within society. Inclusivity and adaptability are key principles in this regard, allowing traditions to evolve and remain relevant while still respecting their core principles.

Government is tasked with preserving cultural heritage, promoting cultural education, and maintaining legal frameworks that protect tradition. Through these efforts, it contributes to the continuity and vitality of tradition in an ever-changing world.

b) Education: Transmitting Cultural Values

Within the spectrum of institutions entrusted with the guardianship of tradition, education holds a unique and pivotal role. It serves as the primary conduit through which cultural values, heritage, and the wisdom of the past are transmitted to the younger generations, ensuring the continuity of a society.

Education has the noble responsibility to impart a deep appreciation for a society's cultural heritage, serving as a bridge between the past and the future, where the stories, customs, and values of previous generations find their way into the hearts and minds of the youth.

Cultural values are a foundational element of tradition, and education acts as the vessel through which these values are instilled. In schools and educational institutions, students are exposed to the moral and ethical principles that underpin their culture. They learn about the importance of respect, compassion, and responsibility, all of which are integral to the preservation of tradition.

Moreover, education offers the opportunity to explore and celebrate cultural diversity. It provides a platform for individuals to learn about the traditions and values of different cultures, fostering tolerance and appreciation for the richness of human heritage. In doing so, education not only transmits one's own cultural values but also encourages a broader understanding of traditions worldwide.

In today's interconnected world, education also plays a crucial role in ensuring that tradition remains relevant and adaptable. While the core values of tradition endure, the means of transmitting them can evolve. Technology, for instance, has provided new avenues for preserving and sharing cultural heritage, and education can harness these tools to reach wider audiences and engage younger generations.

In the face of rapid globalization and cultural homogenization, there is a risk that tradition may be diluted or overshadowed: from this perspective, education must strike a balance between preserving tradition and preparing individuals to survive in a changing world.

c) Religion: The Moral Compass of Society

In the realm of conservative sociology, religion is a cornerstone institution, revered for its function as the ethical lodestar of society, offering not only spiritual guidance but also a robust ethical framework that molds the moral fabric of communities.

At its essence, religion provides a sense of purpose and significance to individuals within society. It addresses fundamental inquiries concerning the nature of existence, the meaning of life, and the human condition. In doing so, it instills a sense of purpose that transcends the material world and forges a profound connection between individuals and their spiritual beliefs.

Religion also plays a central role in shaping individuals' comprehension of right and wrong. It furnishes a set of ethical directives and moral principles that steer human conduct. These guidelines impart a sense of clarity in a complex world, aiding individuals in navigating the moral quandaries they encounter. Through religious teachings, individuals cultivate a robust moral compass, which not only influences their personal behavior but also contributes to the overarching ethical framework of society.

As well, religion nurtures a sense of community and belonging. Houses of worship and religious congregations serve as hubs of social cohesion, uniting individuals who share common convictions and values. These communities provide a wellspring of support, reciprocal aid, and social integration, reinforcing the bonds between individuals and their allegiance to shared moral tenets.

Religion also functions as a fount of ethical counsel in times of uncertainty and moral ambiguity. When individuals confront intricate ethical choices or moral dilemmas, they frequently turn to their religious beliefs and teachings for guidance. Religion provides a wellspring of solace and direction, offering resolutions to questions of morality that may be challenging to discern elsewhere.

However, it's vital to recognize that the role of religion in shaping the moral compass of society is not devoid of intricacies. Distinct religious traditions may present differing viewpoints on ethical matters, leading to diverse interpretations and convictions within a society. This multiplicity can be a source of enrichment and strain alike, underscoring the significance of respectful dialogue and comprehension among individuals of divergent faiths.

In conclusion, religion, as perceived through the perspective of conservative sociology, operates as the ethical compass of society. It furnishes an ethical framework, ethical directives, a sense of purpose, and a wellspring of moral counsel for individuals. By shaping individuals' perception of right and wrong, nurturing community, and imparting ethical clarity, religion makes a substantial contribution to the ethical foundation of society.

9

CONSERVATIVE CRITIQUE OF SOCIOLOGICAL PERSPECTIVES

a) Liberalism and Conservatism: Clash of Ideologies; b) Critiquing Progressive Sociological Theories; c) Examining the Strengths and Weaknesses of Conservative Sociology

a) Liberalism and Conservatism: Clash of Ideologies

Liberalism and conservatism represent two distinct and often contrasting ideologies that have shaped political and social discourse for centuries. This clash of ideologies reflects fundamental differences in their beliefs, values, and approaches to governance.

At the core of liberalism lies a commitment to individual liberties and rights. Liberals champion the idea that individuals should have the freedom to make their own choices, pursue their own interests, and express their own beliefs. They advocate for limited government intervention in personal and economic matters, emphasizing the importance of a free market and minimal state interference. Liberalism often aligns with progressive social values, supporting initiatives aimed at social equality, civil rights, and environmental protection.

Conversely, conservatism places a premium on tradition, stability, and order. Conservatives argue that societal values and institutions have evolved over time for a reason and should be preserved. They tend to be skeptical of rapid change and advocate for a cautious approach to social transformation. Conservatism values established institutions, such as the family, religion, and community, as essential pillars of social cohesion. In terms of governance, conservatives often favor a limited government role in people's lives but may be more inclined to support government intervention in moral and social issues.

The clash between liberalism and conservatism is most evident in their differing views on the role of the state. Liberals often advocate for an active government that plays a role in addressing social inequalities, protecting civil liberties, and regulating markets. They believe that the government can be a force for positive change and social justice. In contrast, conservatives tend to be more skeptical of government intervention, emphasizing the importance of individual responsibility and the potential dangers of an overreaching state.

These ideologies also diverge on issues such as economic policy, immigration, environmental regulation, and foreign policy. Liberalism tends to favor progressive taxation, open immigration policies, strong environmental protections, and international cooperation. Conservatism, on the other hand, may support lower taxes, stricter immigration controls, a more measured approach to environmental regulation, and a focus on national sovereignty in foreign affairs.

While liberalism and conservatism often clash, it's important to recognize that these ideologies exist on a spectrum, and individuals may hold a mix of liberal and conservative views on different issues. Moreover, the clash of ideologies can be a source of healthy debate and compromise in democratic societies, leading to policies that balance individual freedoms with societal stability and progress.

b) Critiquing Progressive Sociological Theories

Conservative sociology provides a critical evaluation of progressive sociological theories that emphasize social change, identity politics, and the deconstruction of traditional societal structures. This critical examination is rooted in a different set of values and principles that prioritize tradition, stability, and the preservation of established social norms.

One key aspect of the conservative critique centers on the rapid pace of social change advocated by progressive theories. Progressive sociological perspectives often champion radical transformations in areas such as gender roles, family structures, and cultural norms. Conservative sociology questions the wisdom of such rapid change, arguing that it can disrupt the stability of communities and erode the values that have historically provided a sense of order and identity.

Identity politics, a central element of many progressive theories, also faces scrutiny from conservative sociology. While acknowledging the importance of recognizing and addressing historical injustices and inequalities, conservatives may argue that an exclusive focus on group identities can foster tribalism and division within society. They may contend that a more inclusive approach that emphasizes shared values and commonalities can be a more effective path to unity.

Conservative sociology also critiques the deconstruction of traditional societal structures and institutions. Progressivism often challenges established institutions such as family, religion, and community, advocating for more flexible and diverse forms of social organization. Conservatives argue that these traditional institutions have played a crucial role in promoting social cohesion and passing down cultural values, and their rapid deconstruction may lead to a sense of disorientation and loss of identity.

Another facet of the conservative critique relates to the role of government in implementing progressive changes. Progressive theories often call for extensive government intervention to address social inequalities and promote social justice. Conservative sociology, while acknowledging the need for government to maintain order and justice, may express concerns about the potential for an overreaching state that infringes on individual freedoms and disrupts the natural order of society.

In essence, conservative sociology offers a counterbalance to progressive sociological theories by emphasizing the importance of tradition, community, and stability. While acknowledging the value of addressing social issues and injustices, conservative sociologists argue for a more cautious and measured approach that balances the pursuit of progress with the preservation of core values and societal order. The clash between these contrasting perspectives contributes to ongoing debates within the field of sociology and shapes the trajectory of social change in society.

Critiquing progressive sociological theories involves a nuanced examination of their underlying assumptions, methodologies, and practical implications. While these theories have made valuable contributions to our understanding of social issues and have driven positive social change, they are not exempt from critical scrutiny.

One common critique revolves around the potential oversimplification of complex social phenomena within progressive theories. Critics argue that these theories often focus on systemic factors, such as structural inequalities and discrimination, while downplaying the significance of individual agency and personal responsibility. This criticism contends that such an emphasis on structural determinism may not fully capture the intricate interplay between individual choices and societal contexts.

Another aspect of critique centers on the feasibility and effectiveness of proposed solutions within progressive sociological theories. While these theories advocate for comprehensive social reforms and government interventions to address systemic issues, critics argue that these solutions may sometimes be overly idealistic or impractical. They suggest that the real-world implementation of such reforms can face logistical challenges and unintended consequences that require careful consideration.

Critiques of progressive sociological theories also extend to questions of cultural relativism and the universal applicability of certain concepts. Critics argue that these theories may not adequately account for cultural variations and may sometimes impose Western-centric frameworks on non-Western societies, potentially leading to misunderstandings and misinterpretations of social dynamics.

The emphasis on victimhood and oppression within some progressive theories also must draw criticism, because a fixation on victim narratives may inadvertently encourage a culture of victimization, potentially undermining self-empowerment among marginalized individuals.

c) Examining the Strengths and Weaknesses of Conservative Sociology

Like any comprehensive framework, conservative sociology presents both merits and challenges that merit careful consideration.

In terms of strengths, conservative sociology places a notable emphasis on the preservation of tradition and cultural values. This commitment recognizes the significance of continuity and stability in society, as well as the importance of passing down cultural heritage from one generation to the next. By upholding tradition, this perspective helps communities maintain a sense of identity and shared values, contributing to a sense of belonging and stability.

Another strength lies in the recognition of traditional institutions like family, religion, and local communities as essential for social cohesion. These institutions serve as vital sources of support, mutual assistance, and belonging, collectively contributing to the overall well-being of individuals and communities. Conservative sociology underscores the importance of these institutions in maintaining social order and a sense of interconnectedness.

Moreover, conservative thought advocates for a cautious approach to social change, supporting evaluations of potential consequences of rapid change. This measured approach can help mitigate unforeseen negative effects and promote a smoother transition during periods of transformation.

Conservative sociology places also a strong emphasis on individuals, encouraging people to take control of their lives and make responsible choices, fostering a sense of personal agency and accountability.

On the flip side, conservative sociology also presents certain weaknesses. Critics argue that it can be resistant to necessary progress and social reforms, particularly in addressing issues like inequality, discrimination, and social injustices. This resistance may hinder efforts to improve societal conditions and rectify systemic problems.

The emphasis on tradition and stability can lead to inflexibility in adapting to changing societal norms and values. This rigidity may marginalize or exclude individuals and groups who do not conform to traditional norms, potentially stifling diversity and inclusivity.

In some cases, conservative sociology may promote exclusive social structures or hierarchies that marginalize certain segments of society. This exclusivity can perpetuate inequalities and limit opportunities for individuals who do not fit within traditional frameworks.

Critics also argue that conservative sociology may not adequately account for cultural diversity and may impose a singular set of values and norms on a diverse society. This can lead to the neglect or suppression of cultural pluralism, hindering the recognition of different perspectives and experiences.

Additionally, in a rapidly changing world, the cautious and measured approach of conservative sociology may be perceived as insufficient in addressing urgent societal challenges. Issues such as technological advancements and globalization may require more proactive and adaptive responses to effectively address complex and pressing problems.

In summary, conservative sociology offers strengths in preserving tradition, promoting community cohesion, and emphasizing individual responsibility. However, it also faces criticisms for potential resistance to progress, inflexibility, exclusivity, and potential ineffectiveness in addressing rapid social change. These strengths and weaknesses contribute to ongoing debates within the field of sociology and shape discussions about how best to address complex social issues and adapt to evolving societal dynamics.

10
APPLICATIONS OF CONSERVATIVE SOCIOLOGY

a) Conservative Sociology in Policy-making; b) Contributions to Social and Cultural Analysis; c) Implications for Social and Community Development

a) Conservative Sociology in Policy-making

The application of conservative sociology in policy-making is a complex and nuanced process that involves drawing insights and principles from this sociological perspective to inform government policies. While it is not the sole determinant of policy decisions, conservative sociology can offer valuable perspectives and considerations that can shape policy formulation.

One of the key aspects of applying conservative sociology in policy-making is the emphasis on preserving tradition and cultural values. This perspective can influence policy decisions related to cultural preservation, heritage protection, and the promotion of traditional values within society. Policymakers may craft initiatives and programs aimed at preserving historical landmarks, traditions, and cultural practices to ensure their continuity and relevance.

Conservative sociology also recognizes the importance of traditional family structures and local communities in fostering social cohesion. In the realm of policy-making, this perspective can guide decisions related to family and community support. Policymakers may develop programs that strengthen family bonds, encourage community engagement, and promote mutual support networks. These policies may encompass a range of initiatives, from supporting family stability through parental leave to providing family counseling services.

A cautious approach to social change can have a significant impact on policy decisions too. Policymakers may consider the potential consequences and unintended side effects of rapid changes when crafting policies. This perspective can lead to a more deliberate and measured approach to policy implementation, allowing for continuous evaluation and adjustment to ensure that societal stability is maintained.

The emphasis on individual responsibility and self-reliance within conservative sociology informs policy decisions related to welfare and social assistance programs. Policymakers may strive to strike a balance between providing necessary support to those in need and encouraging individual initiative and accountability. This balance aims to empower individuals to take charge of their lives while ensuring a safety net for those facing hardships.

Moreover, the recognition of the significance of local communities in conservative sociology can inspire policies that decentralize decision-making. Policymakers may explore approaches that grant more autonomy to local governments and community organizations, allowing them to develop solutions that align with their unique values and needs. This decentralized approach aims to empower communities to address their specific challenges effectively.

Conservative sociology's emphasis on traditional moral values can also influence policies related to education, media, and public ethics. Policymakers may consider approaches that align with conservative values when addressing concerns related to media content, educational curriculum, or public displays of morality.

Lastly, the overarching theme of balancing stability and progress within conservative sociology can guide economic and social policy decisions. Policymakers, while striving for progress and innovation, may seek to maintain a level of stability and continuity that provides a sense of security and order to society.

Applying conservative sociology in policy-making could be a complex endeavor that draws from various sociological perspectives, but it can offer a unique lens through which policymakers can view and address societal challenges.

b) Contributions to Social and Cultural Analysis

The application of conservative sociology to social and cultural analysis offers a distinctive perspective that contributes to a more comprehensive understanding of societal dynamics. While it may not provide the sole perspective through which to examine these complex issues, conservative sociology brings valuable insights and considerations to the table.

One notable contribution of conservative sociology to social and cultural analysis, as repeatedly expressed, is the emphasis on the preservation of traditional values. This perspective could encourage scholars and analysts to delve into the historical roots of cultural practices, norms, and institutions. By studying the evolution of tradition, researchers can gain a deeper appreciation for the role these elements play in shaping society and providing a sense of identity and continuity.

Also the recognition of the importance of traditional family structures and local communities is instrumental in cultural analysis. This perspective prompts researchers to explore the ways in which these traditional institutions influence norms and practices.

Conservative sociology's cautious approach to

social change is another valuable contribution, leading scholars to critically examine the consequences of rapid cultural shifts and the potential challenges they pose. This perspective prompts researchers to consider the ways in which cultural transformations impact individual identities, and community cohesion.

The emphasis on individual responsibility and self-reliance within conservative sociology also informs cultural analysis. Researchers may investigate how these principles influence cultural attitudes toward personal agency, accountability, and self-determination. This lens can shed light on cultural narratives of self-reliance and the role of the individual within the larger societal context.

Moreover, conservative sociology's focus on community-based solutions contributes to an understanding of how culture is shaped and maintained at the local level. By studying the dynamics of local communities and their role in cultural preservation, researchers can gain insights into the mechanisms through which cultural practices are sustained and adapted over time.

In summary, conservative sociology offers valuable contributions to social and cultural analysis by emphasizing tradition, family, community, cautious change, individual responsibility, and moral values. While not without its critics and limitations, this perspective enriches the broader discourse on culture and society by providing a distinct vantage point from which to explore the complexities of human culture and its evolution. It encourages a more holistic approach to cultural analysis that encompasses both continuity and change.

c) Implications for Social and Community Development

The application of conservative sociology to social and community development carries profound implications for how policies and initiatives are designed and implemented to secure the well-being and stability of societies and local communities. It's a perspective that prioritizes tradition, family, community, and a cautious approach to change, all of which inform various aspects of social and community development.

One of the key implications is the preservation of community identity. Conservative sociology underscores the importance of local communities as fundamental units of social organization. In the context of social and community development, this perspective places a significant emphasis on the need to strengthen community identities and recognize the uniqueness of each one of them.

Family stability is another critical dimension influenced by conservative sociology. This perspective advocates for policies that help family cohesion, such as offering support services, promoting parenting skills, and addressing issues that can disrupt family stability. By prioritizing family units, conservative sociology contributes to the overall social stability of communities.

The cautious approach to change advocated by conservative sociology also has implications for social and community development. It prompts policymakers and development practitioners to carefully consider the potential consequences of rapid change within communities. Rather than imposing abrupt transformations, a more measured approach is favored, allowing communities to adapt at their own pace while preserving their core values and structures.

Community-based solutions are a central tenet of conservative sociology: policymakers are encouraged to engage local communities in the decision-making process, respecting their unique needs and preferences. This participatory approach fosters a sense of ownership and empowerment within communities, ultimately leading to more effective and sustainable development outcomes.

Lastly, we must consider the moral and ethical dimensions of social and community development, calling for initiatives that align with traditional moral values and ethical principles. Efforts are made to ensure that development projects respect the ethical foundations of communities and uphold the cultural values that guide their behavior and decisions.

In conclusion, the application of conservative sociology to social and community development emphasizes the preservation of community identity, family stability, a cautious approach to change, individual responsibility, community-based solutions, and the alignment of development efforts with moral and ethical values. These implications contribute to the creation of more culturally sensitive, community-centered, and sustainable development strategies that promote the well-being and stability of societies and local communities.

11
FUTURE DIRECTIONS AND CHALLENGES

a) Adapting Conservative Sociology to Changing Times; b) Addressing Critiques and Expanding Research; c) The Relevance of Conservative Sociology in a Dynamic World

a) Adapting Conservative Sociology to Changing Times

While our perspective is rooted in tradition, stability, and the preservation of established norms, it cannot remain static in a world marked by rapid technological advancements, evolving social structures, and shifting cultural values. Adapting conservative sociology to changing times involves addressing several critical considerations.

One of the foremost challenges is striking a balance between tradition and innovation. While conservative sociology values the preservation of traditional values and practices, it must also acknowledge that some aspects of society are in a state of continual evolution. This necessitates a willingness to engage with and adapt to new ideas, technologies, and social dynamics without compromising core principles.

In an increasingly diverse and multicultural world, conservative sociology faces the task of being inclusive and respectful of different cultural perspectives. Adapting to changing times requires recognizing that traditional values can coexist with the values of various cultural groups. It entails an openness to dialogue and understanding across cultural boundaries while maintaining a commitment to the preservation of core cultural values.

The pursuit of social justice and the addressing of issues related to inequality, discrimination, and systemic injustices are central concerns in contemporary society. Adapting conservative sociology means engaging with these issues in a meaningful way. This may involve reevaluating how traditional principles can be applied to promote social justice and address historical inequalities without compromising the core tenets of conservatism.

Technological advancements and their impact on society present another challenge. Conservative sociology needs to navigate the rapidly changing landscape of digital communication, artificial intelligence, and automation. It requires an examination of how these technologies influence social interactions, employment patterns, and privacy concerns while upholding the principles of individual responsibility and community cohesion.

In an era of globalization and cultural pluralism, conservative sociology must engage with the challenges and opportunities presented by an interconnected world. It involves understanding how traditional values can coexist with a diverse and global society while preserving cultural identities and values.

In addressing these challenges, conservative sociology should remain open to critical dialogue, interdisciplinary collaboration, and a willingness to adapt its perspectives to the changing times. It must find ways to preserve core principles while responding thoughtfully and constructively to the complex issues facing contemporary society. Adapting conservative sociology to changing times is a dynamic and ongoing process that requires a delicate balance between tradition and adaptation.

b) Addressing Critiques and Expanding Research

One of the most pressing challenges for conservative thought is addressing the criticisms that have been directed towards it. Critics argue that it can sometimes be seen as resistant to societal progress and social reforms, particularly when it comes to issues of inequality, discrimination, and social injustices. To maintain its credibility and influence, conservative sociology must engage constructively with these critiques.

Expanding the research focus is also imperative for the future of conservative sociology. Traditionally, the field has concentrated on topics such as family, community, and tradition. However, the evolving dynamics of society demand a broader research agenda. Researchers should delve into emerging issues, including the profound impact of technology on society and the shifting landscape of family structures. By diversifying research topics, conservative sociology can stay attuned to contemporary challenges and remain relevant in an ever-changing world.

In the pursuit of expanding research, comparative studies should play a significant role. These studies can analyze the effectiveness of conservative policies and approaches in different cultural and societal contexts. By examining how conservative principles manifest and impact society across various regions and demographics, researchers can gain valuable insights into the versatility and adaptability of conservative sociology.

Policy evaluation is another avenue that holds great potential for conservative sociology. Researchers should rigorously assess the outcomes of policies influenced by conservative principles. These may include policies related to family support, community development, education, and more. Evaluating the actual effectiveness of these policies in achieving their intended outcomes is essential for evidence-based decision-making and refining conservative sociological perspectives.

Collaboration with scholars from other disciplines is increasingly important. Engaging in interdisciplinary approaches by collaborating with experts in ethics, philosophy, political science, economics, and other fields can lead to innovative solutions to complex societal challenges. Cross-disciplinary dialogue can foster a more holistic understanding of societal dynamics and encourage the integration of diverse perspectives.

Moreover, empirical research should be embraced alongside theoretical foundations. While conservative sociology boasts strong theoretical underpinnings, empirical studies can provide concrete evidence and data-driven insights into societal phenomena.

Empirical research enhances the field's credibility and enables it to contribute to sociological discussions.

c) The Relevance of Conservative Sociology in a Dynamic World

In an era characterized by constant social, technological, and cultural shifts, the field must grapple with several vital considerations to develop its influence.

It's important to recognize that the field of sociology is not monolithic, and different scholars and perspectives may have varying views on how to engage with social transformations, including issues related, for example, to gender equality or LGBTQ+ rights.

Indeed, a fundamental tenet of conservative sociology is the desire to protect and preserve tradition in a dynamic and ever-changing world. This perspective values the wisdom, stability, and continuity that tradition offers to society. It asserts that tradition serves as a valuable anchor in times of rapid social, cultural, and technological transformations.

Conservative scholars may argue that particular issues, such as same-sex couples raising children or transgender rights, represent departures from traditional understandings of marriage and gender roles and have a disruptive impact on societies. These changes challenge the stability and continuity of society even on a mere political level as, for instance, contentious legal and policy debates divide people and consume resources and attention that might be directed toward other societal issues.

With regard to certain topics, such as those mentioned above, we argue that the emphasis on individual freedom and agency can lead to social fragmentation and disorder. When individuals prioritize their personal choices and desires over collective values and responsibilities, it can potentially undermine the cohesion and shared identity of a community or society. Conservative sociologists may assert that there are instances where it becomes necessary to uphold and reinforce social structures, even if it means limiting individual freedoms to some extent. This perspective argues that such measures are essential to maintain a sense of continuity, order, and shared values in society.

The goal of Conservative Sociology is to contribute to a broader societal dialogue by presenting alternative viewpoints and highlighting the significance of tradition and stability in understanding and addressing contemporary challenges.

This is just an example of how conservative sociology aims to provide an alternative perspective to mainstream viewpoints, which often lean toward liberalism and progressivism. This alternative viewpoint is rooted in traditional values, stability, and a preference for continuity over rapid societal change. In the end, it's also important to add that conservative sociology encompasses a range of perspectives and approaches within its framework. While some conservative sociologists may prioritize the preservation of tradition, others may explore ways to adapt traditional values to changing societal contexts. The field's overall goal is to contribute to a rich and multifaceted sociological landscape that considers the complexities of social issues from a conservative standpoint.

12
THE ENDURING RELEVANCE OF CONSERVATIVE SOCIOLOGY

a) Summary of Key Findings; b) Importance of Traditional Values in Understanding Society; c) Moving Forward with a Conservative Sociological Perspective

a) Summary of Key Findings

Conservative sociology, while rooted in tradition, has demonstrated its enduring relevance in addressing the complex sociological dynamics of the modern world.

One of the key findings is that conservative sociology places a strong emphasis on tradition, stability, and the preservation of established values. It recognizes tradition as a pillar of social cohesion, providing a moral compass that shapes individual behavior and fosters a sense of collective responsibility. Traditional values, such as respect for authority, family, and community, contribute significantly to social stability and cohesion. These values prioritize the welfare of the group over individual desires, promoting cooperation and mutual support within communities.

Conservative sociology also views society as an organic entity, akin to a living organism. This perspective highlights the interconnectedness of social institutions and the importance of maintaining balance and order within society. Social cohesion emerges as a central concept, emphasizing the need for shared values, stable family structures, and strong local communities to ensure societal stability.

The traditional family structure, according to conservative sociology, serves as a foundational unit of society. While acknowledging the need for flexibility and adaptation to accommodate changing societal norms and individual preferences, conservative sociology underscores the family's role in providing stability, nurturing environments for children, and passing down cultural values.

Local communities, regarded as fundamental units of social organization, offer vital sources of social support, fostering a sense of belonging, identity, and mutual assistance. They play a crucial role in maintaining a sense of rootedness and connection to one's surroundings, particularly in an increasingly interconnected world.

Furthermore, conservative sociology recognizes the role of hierarchy in social organization. Hierarchy establishes clear lines of authority, facilitating decision-making processes and the implementation of collective goals. It provides structure, accountability, and specialization, ensuring the efficient functioning and coordination of social systems.

The Rule of Law, upheld by conservative sociology, serves as a mainspring of social order, offering stability and predictability within society. It emphasizes the importance of adherence to established norms and the role of institutions in upholding tradition and order.

Despite its enduring relevance, conservative

sociology faces challenges in adapting to changing times. These include addressing critiques related to social progress, embracing technological advancements, engaging with intersectionality and diversity, and fostering dialogue across disciplinary boundaries. To remain pertinent, conservative sociology must evolve while staying true to its core principles, actively contributing to contemporary sociological discussions, and adopting a forward-looking approach.

b) Importance of Traditional Values in Understanding Society

The enduring relevance of conservative sociology becomes particularly apparent when we consider the importance it places on traditional values in understanding society. This perspective acknowledges that tradition, as a repository of accumulated wisdom and collective experience, plays a fundamental role in shaping social dynamics.

Traditional values encompass a wide range of principles, including respect for authority, honor, duty, loyalty, family, and community. These values serve as a moral compass, guiding individual behavior and promoting a sense of collective responsibility. They provide a foundational framework upon which societies are built, offering stability and continuity in an ever-changing world.

At the heart of this perspective is the recognition that traditional values are not merely relics of the past but living forces that continue to influence contemporary society. They help establish social norms and expectations, guiding individuals in their interactions and relationships. By doing so, they foster a sense of shared responsibility, emphasizing the importance of fulfilling duties and obligations towards family, community, and society at large.

One of the most significant roles of traditional

values is their contribution to social cohesion. These values prioritize the welfare of the group over individual desires, fostering cooperation, mutual support, and solidarity within communities. They encourage individuals to contribute to the common good and help establish a sense of interdependence among community members.

In a broader context, the importance of traditional values in understanding society is evident in their influence on various social institutions. Traditional family structures, for instance, are seen as foundational units of society, providing stability, nurturing environments for children, and the transmission of cultural values..

Conservative sociology recognizes the need for flexibility and adaptation within the traditional framework to accommodate changing societal norms and individual preferences. It doesn't advocate for rigid adherence to tradition but rather emphasizes the preservation of core values and principles while allowing for responsible evolution.

c) Moving Forward with a Conservative Sociological Perspective

As we conclude our exploration, it becomes evident that this sociological perspective provides valuable insights for understanding and navigating the complexities of contemporary society. Moving forward, it is essential to consider how a conservative sociological perspective can continue to contribute to our understanding of the world and address the challenges of the future.

One of the key takeaways from our discussion is that conservative sociology offers a unique lens through which to view society. It places a strong emphasis on tradition, stability, and the preservation of established values.

In a rapidly changing world marked by technological advancements, shifting cultural norms, and evolving family structures, the conservative sociological perspective offers a sense of continuity and stability. It reminds us of the enduring power of tradition and the importance of preserving core values, even as we adapt to new circumstances.

Conservative sociology is a field that can evolve and adapt to changing times while remaining true to its principles. One of the challenges that conservative sociology faces is the need to address contemporary issues such as inequality, social justice, and technological advancements. Conservative sociologists can contribute meaningfully to these discussions by offering a perspective that values tradition while recognizing the need for responsible evolution.

Additionally, we can play a role in fostering dialogue and collaboration across different sociological perspectives by engaging in constructive debates and finding areas of convergence with other perspectives.

In conclusion, the relevance of conservative sociology lies in its capacity to offer insights into the complexities of contemporary society while upholding traditional values and principles. Moving forward, the field should continue to evolve by actively contributing to discussions about the nature of society and its future. By doing so, conservative sociology can remain a valuable and influential sociological perspective in an ever-changing world.